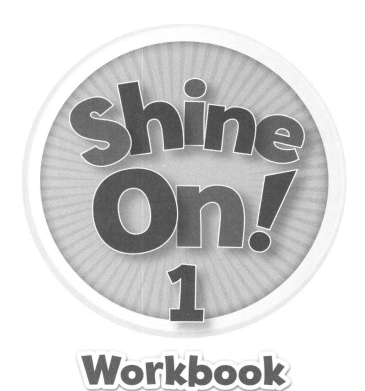

Contents

OXFORD
UNIVERSITY PRESS

1 Color and say the names. Say *Hello*.

Vocabulary Lucy, Jack, Uncle Alex   **Grammar** What's your name? I'm Jack.

1 SB Page 5 | Match and say.

①

②

③

At School

Lesson 1

1 Circle the odd one out. Say.

1.

2.

3.

4.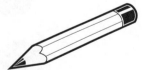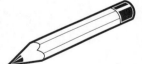

5.

6.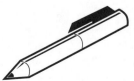

Vocabulary book, pencil, pen, backpack, desk, chair

1 Lesson 2

1 Find and color the •. Say.

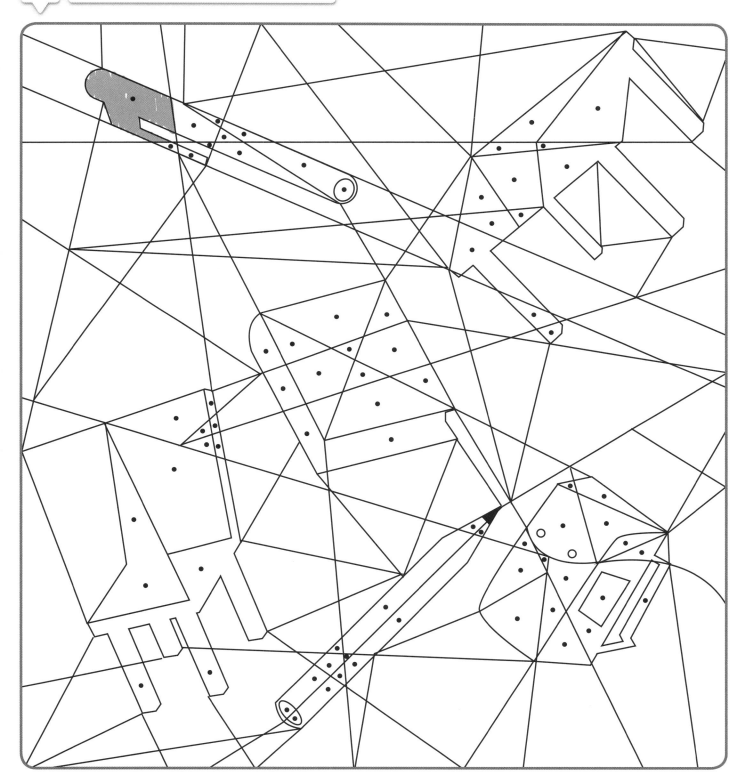

1 SB **Page 10** What's missing? Follow and draw. Then say.

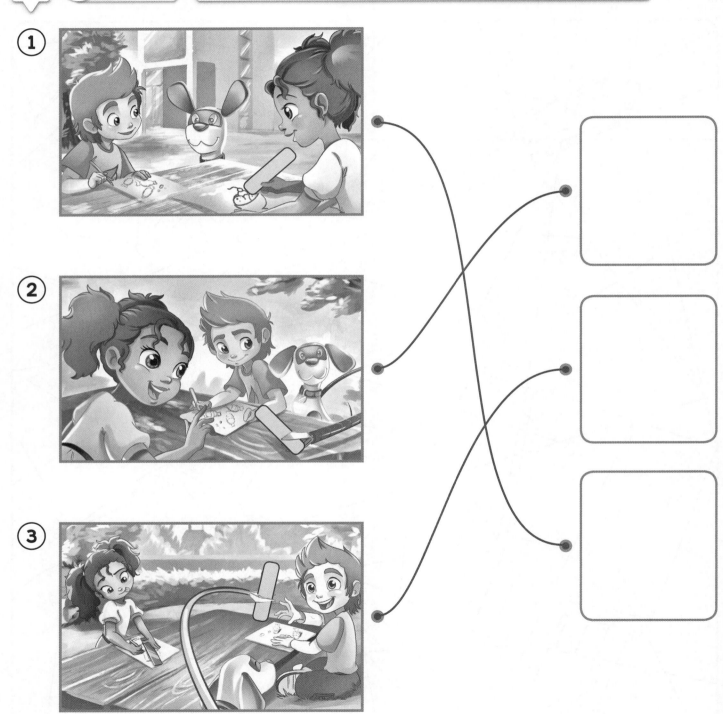

2 What's next? Draw and say.

Everyday English!

3 Look and say.

1 Where are the objects? Match and say.

①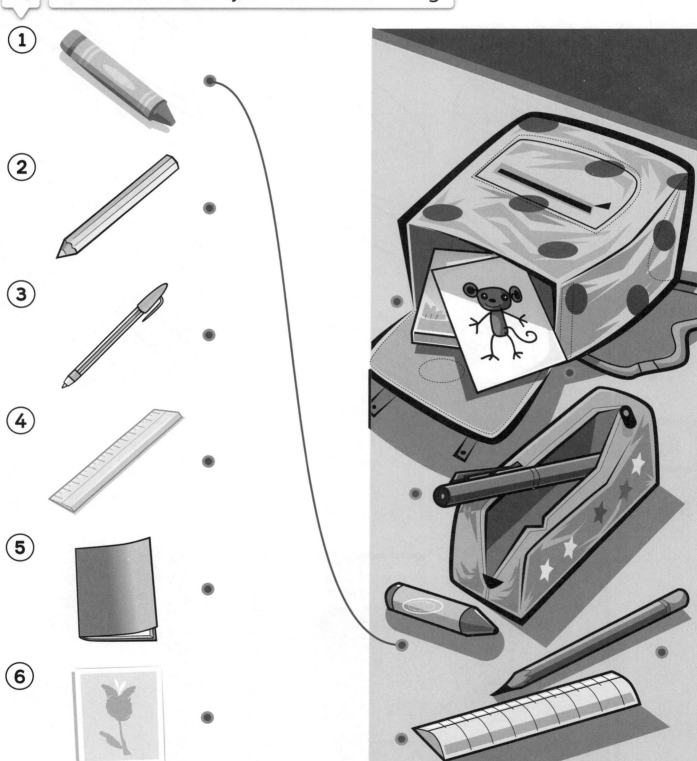

②

③

④

⑤

⑥

1 Trace and say. Make a ✓.

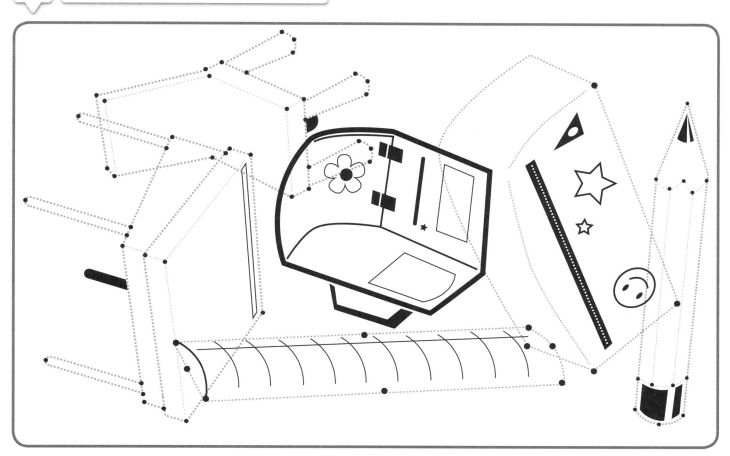

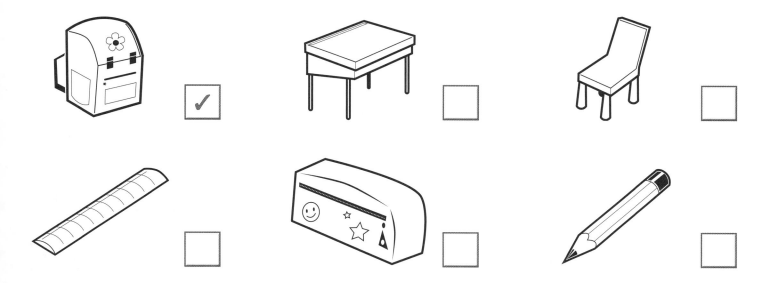

Fun Colors

Lesson 1

1 Color the balloons. Color the picture and say.

Vocabulary yellow, blue, white, red, black, green

1 Color and match.

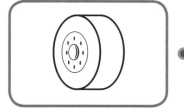

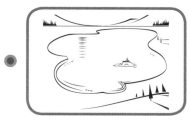

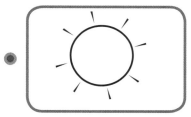

Grammar What color is it? It's white.   11

1 SB Page 18 Color and say.

①

②

③

2 Circle the odd one out. Say the color.

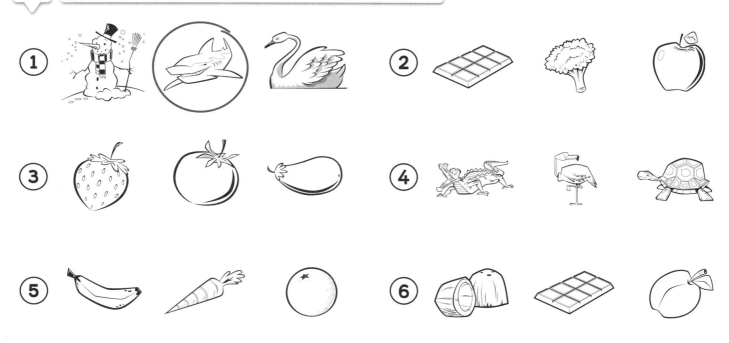

Everyday English!

3 Draw yourself. Show your friend and say.

Look!

Good job!

1 Color and say. Match.

②

③

Vocabulary red, white, yellow, black, gray, orange, pink

1 Color the crayons. Follow and color. Then say.

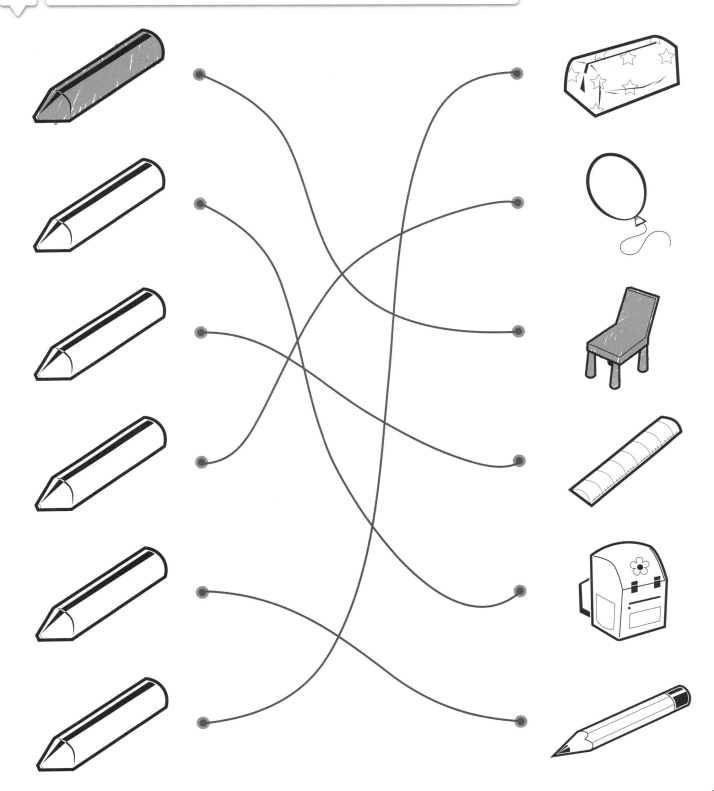

Revision 1

1 Match and say.

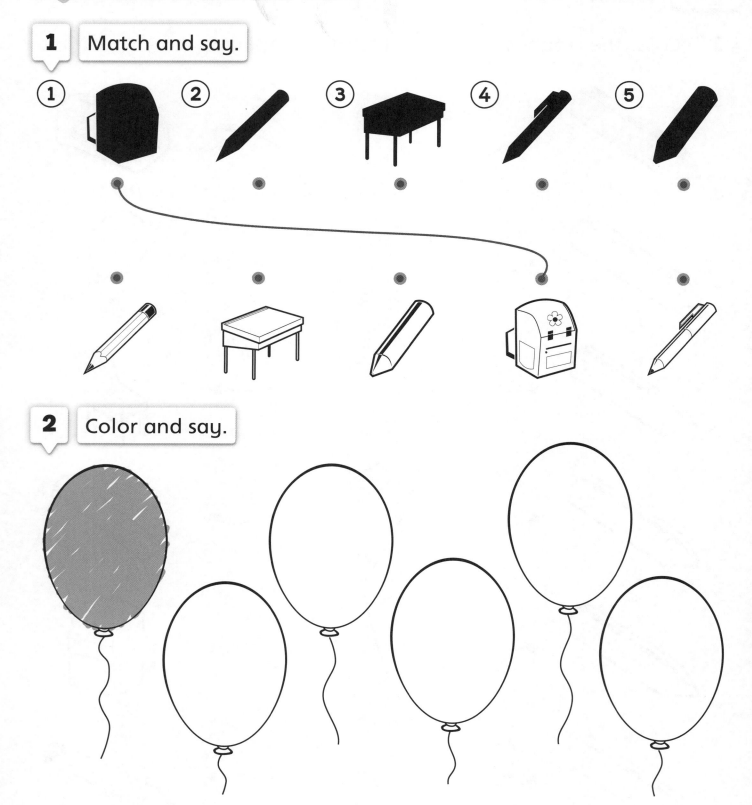

2 Color and say.

3 Trace and say.

1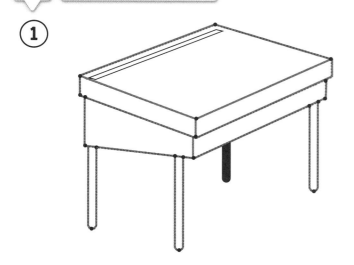

2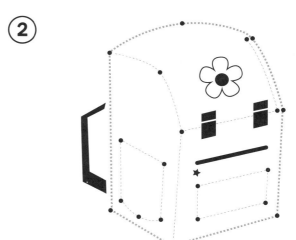

3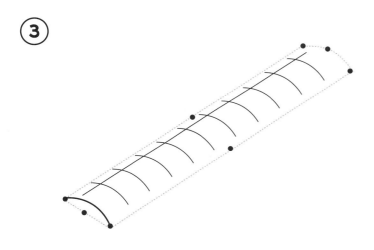

4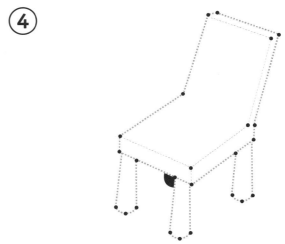

5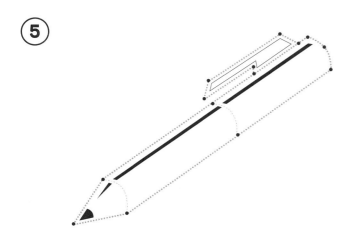

6

Cool Toys!

Lesson 1

1 Match and say.

① 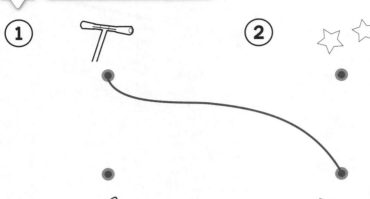　② 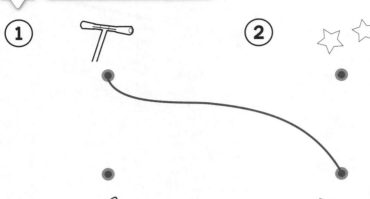　③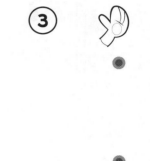

④ 　⑤ 　⑥

　　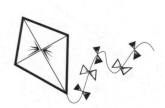

Vocabulary doll, ball, kite, teddy, bike, scooter

1 Draw and color. Say.

①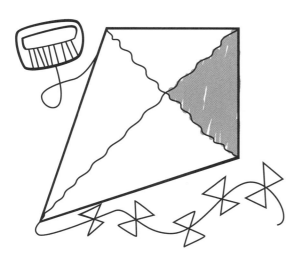

②

③

④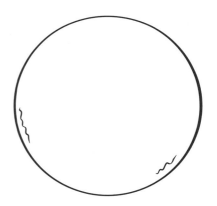

⑤

⑥

1 **SB** **Page 28** What's missing? Match and color. Then say.

①

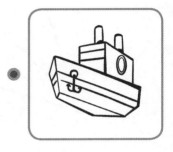

②

③

2 Color the shapes. Color the picture and say.

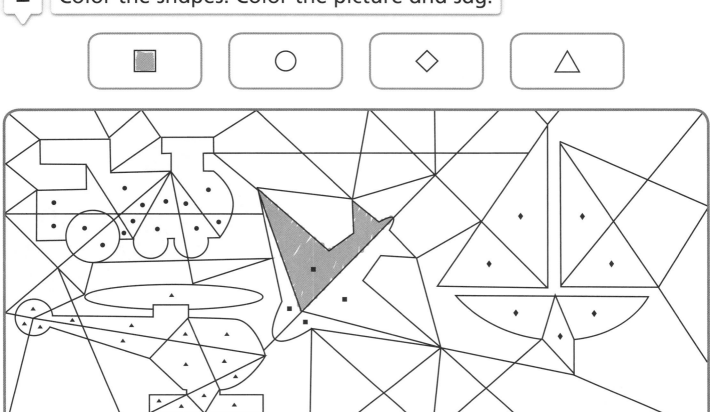

Everyday English!

3 Draw a toy. Say.

It's your turn.

Thanks!

1 Look and circle. Say.

①

②

③

④

3 Review

1 Color the toys. Say.

Let's Count!

1 Trace, count, and match. Color and say.

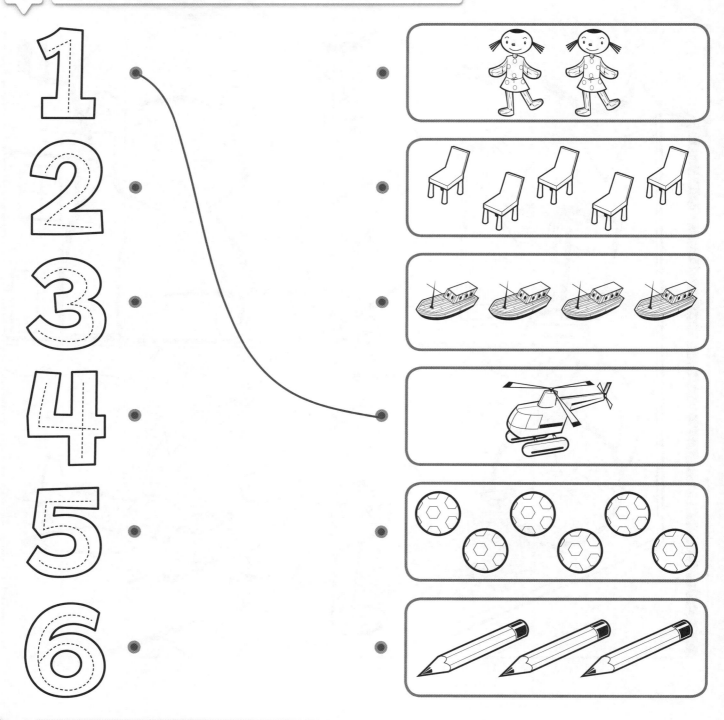

Vocabulary one, two, three, four, five, six

1 Count and write the number. Say.

①
2

②

③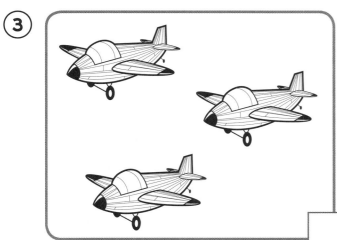

④

⑤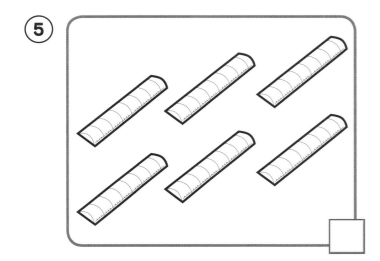

⑥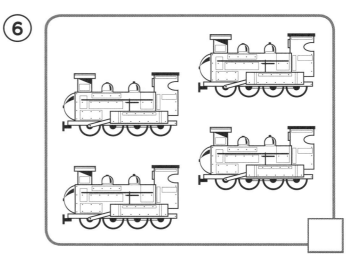

Grammar How many bikes? Two.

25

4 Lesson 3 | Story: Play Store!

1 SB Page 36 | How many? Match. Then say.

①

⑦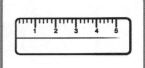

②

2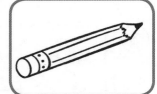

③

6

④

1

2 Count and match. Say.

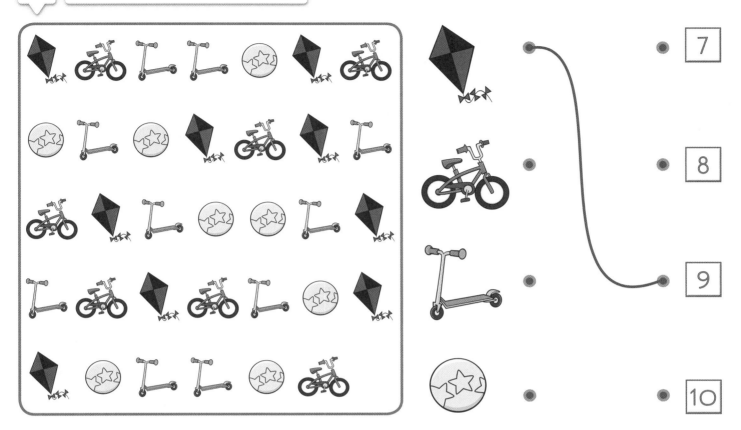

Everyday English!

3 What do they say? Match and say.

Please help.

OK.

Lesson 4 | **Math**

1 Count, draw, and write the number.

① 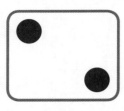 +  =

2 + 3 =

②  +  =

3 + 4 =

③  +  =

5 + 5 =

2 Look and circle. Draw.

 + / =  + / =

Vocabulary plus, equals

1 Follow, count, and circle. Say.

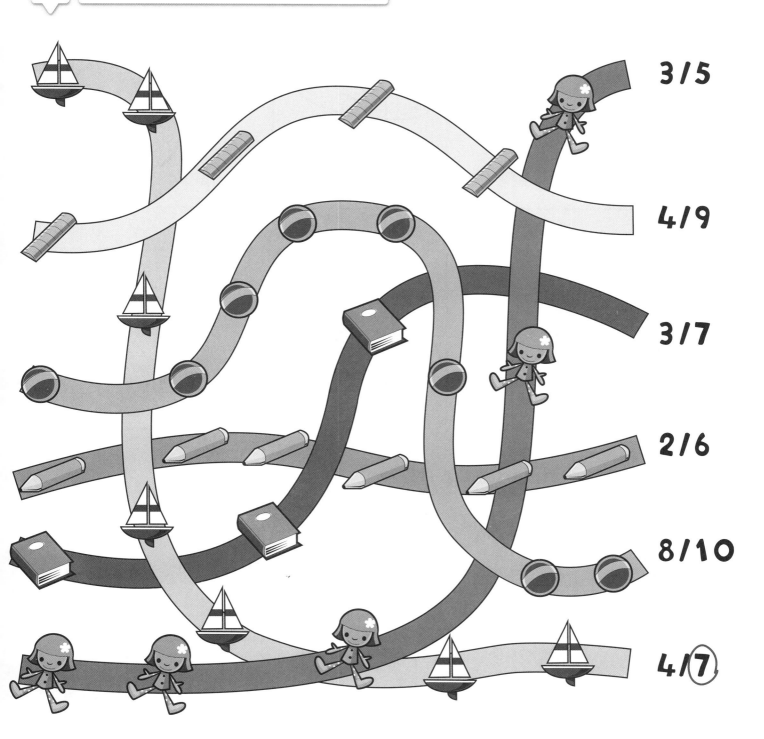

3 / 5

4 / 9

3 / 7

2 / 6

8 / 10

4 / ⑦

Revision 2

1 Draw and say.

①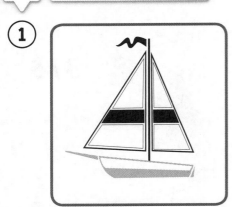

②

③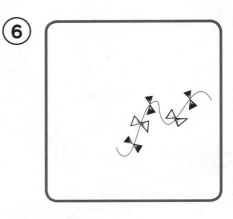

④

⑤

⑥

2 Write the numbers. Say.

1	2	3	___	5

6	___	8	___	10

3 Color the toys. Say.

4 Count and match. Say.

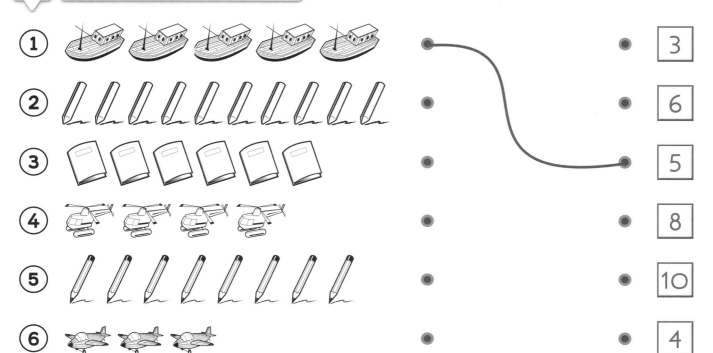

① 3
② 6
③ 5
④ 8
⑤ 10
⑥ 4

My Body

Lesson 1

1 Look and match. Say.

arms •

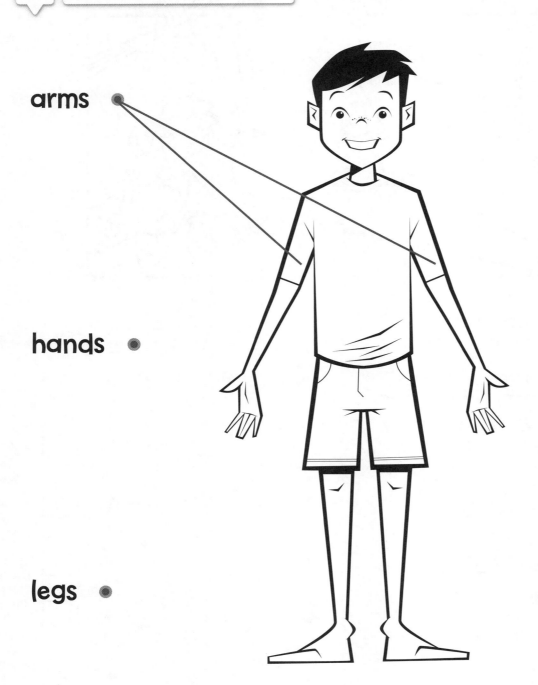

• head

hands •

• fingers

legs •

• feet

Vocabulary arms, head, hands, fingers, legs, feet

1 Look and circle. Say and do.

①  Touch your (legs) / head!

②  Shake your **fingers** / head!

③  Touch your **arms** / **feet**!

④  Shake your **legs** / **hands**!

⑤  Touch your **head** / **feet**!

⑥  Shake your **hands** / **legs**!

1 SB **Page 46** Look, say, and number in order.

2 Look and match. Draw.

1 nose

2 eyes

3 mouth

4 ears

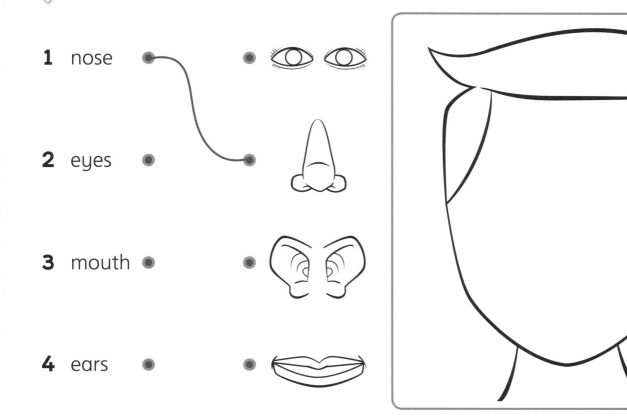

Everyday English!

3 What do they say? Match and say.

I'm sorry.

That's OK.

1 Color the crayons. Follow and color. Then say.

mouth

nose

eyes

ears

2 Draw and color. Say.

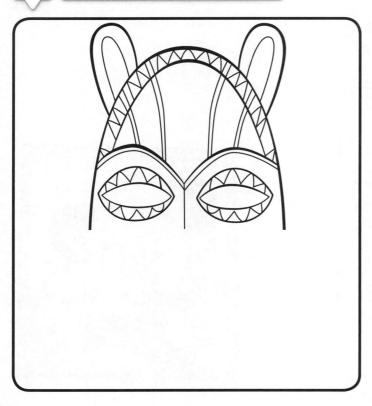

Vocabulary mask

1 Look and number.

1 Shake your head!

2 Touch your eyes!

3 Shake your legs!

4 Touch your nose!

5 Shake your arms!

6 Touch your feet!

 1

6 Animals

1 Look and circle. Say.

lion

hippo

snake

monkey

giraffe

zebra

snake

monkey

hippo

zebra

lion

giraffe

Vocabulary monkey, lion, zebra, snake, giraffe, hippo

1 Match and say.

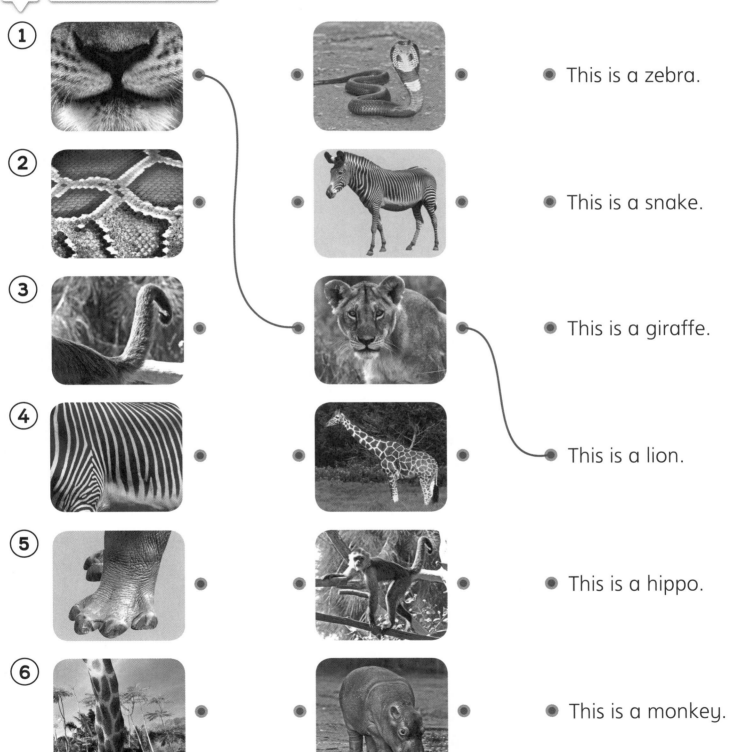

1.
2.
3.
4.
5.
6.

This is a zebra.

This is a snake.

This is a giraffe.

This is a lion.

This is a hippo.

This is a monkey.

1 SB Page 54 What's missing? Follow and draw. Then say.

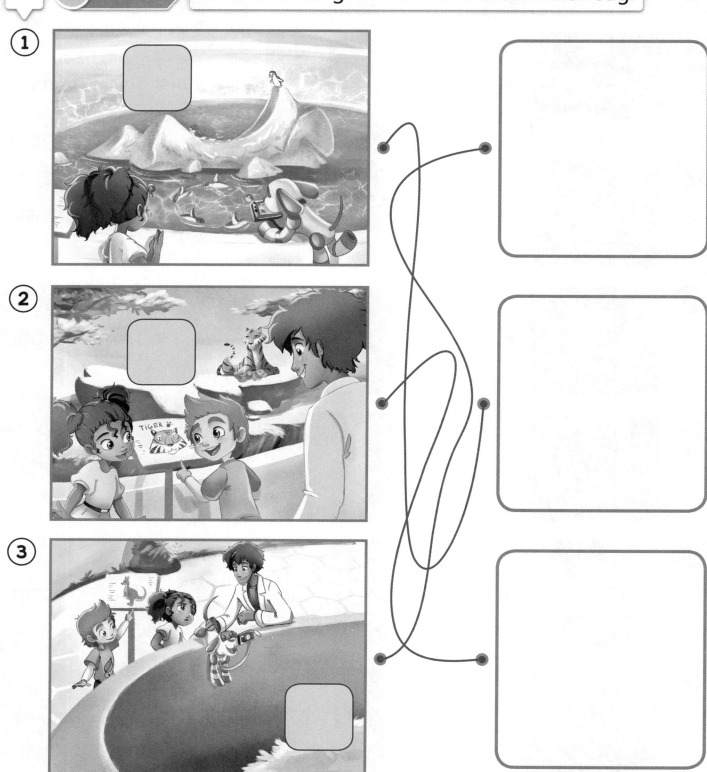

2 Circle the odd one out. Say.

1

2

3

4

Everyday English!

3 What do they say? Match and say.

Watch out!

OK.

1 Circle the baby animals and say.

①  ②

③  ④

2 Match and say.

mouth •

ears •

eyes •

nose •

6 Review

1 Look and say. Find and circle.

① ② ③
④ ⑤ ⑥

Revision 3

1 Match and say.

1 hands

2 head

3 legs

4 nose

5 eyes

6 arms

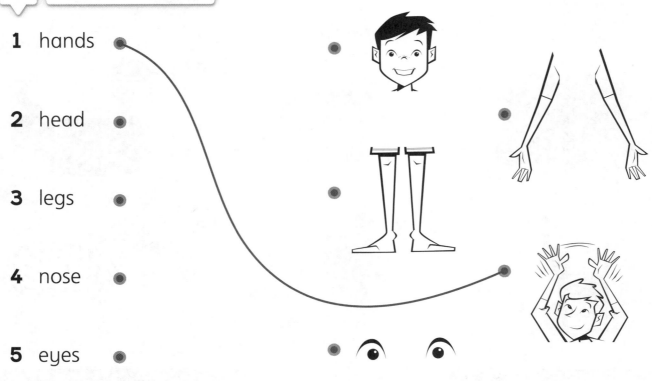

2 Look and number.

1 zebra   2 snake   3 penguin   4 giraffe

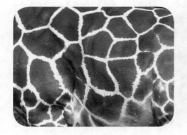         

        1

3 Look and circle. Say.

1  (touch) / shake

2  touch / shake

3  touch / shake

4  touch / shake

4 Match and say.

1

snake

lion

monkey

penguin

hippo

kangaroo

2

3

4

5

6

1 Look and match. Say.

①  ● ──────────● dad

②  ●

③  ● ──────────● sister

④  ● ● mom

⑤  ● ● grandma

⑥  ● ● grandpa

● brother

Vocabulary mom, grandpa, dad, sister, brother, grandma

1 Look and number. Say.

①  ②  ③

④  ⑤  ⑥

This is my brother. ☐

This is my mom. ☐

This is my grandpa. ☐

This is my grandma. 1

This is my dad. ☐

This is my sister. ☐

Grammar Who's this? This is my grandma.   47

1 SB **Page 64** What's missing? Circle and color. Then say.

①

②

③

2 Follow and circle. Say.

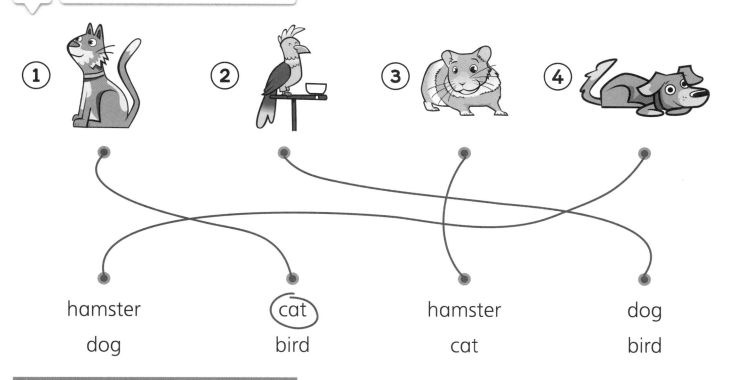

① hamster / dog

② (cat) / bird

③ hamster / cat

④ dog / bird

Everyday English!

3 Look and make a ✓ or an ✗. Say.

How are you?

☐ I'm fine, thank you.

☐ I'm fine, thank you.

1 Look and make a ✓ or an ✗. Say.

This is my family.

1 This is my grandma. ✓

2 This is my mom. ☐

3 This is my brother. ☐

4 This is my dad. ☐

5 This is my grandpa. ☐

6 This is my sister. ☐

7 Review

1 Look and choose. Circle and draw. Then say.

mom   dad   brother   sister   grandma
grandpa   dog   (hamster)   cat

This is my hamster.

Feeling Good

Lesson 1

1 Look and make a ✓ or an ✗. Say.

①

hot ✓

sad ✗

②

sad ☐

happy ☐

③

cold ☐

hungry ☐

④

happy ☐

tired ☐

⑤

hungry ☐

cold ☐

⑥

tired ☐

hot ☐

Vocabulary cold, hot, sad, happy, tired, hungry

Lesson 2

1 Look and match. Say.

①

He's cold.

②

③

She's happy.

She's hungry.

④

He's tired.

⑤

He's hot.

⑥

She's sad.

Grammar He's tired. 53

Lesson 3 | **Story: Happy Day!**

1 | **SB** **Page 72** | Look and circle. Say.

①

hot   tired   fast

②

slow   noisy   sad

③

quiet   tired   hot

④

happy   fast   tired

Look and make a ✓ or an ✗. Say.

1 noisy  ☒ ✗   ☑ ✓

2 quiet ☐   ☐

3 slow ☐   ☐

4 fast   ☐    ☐

Everyday English!

3 What do they say? Match and say.

●   Thanks.

●   You're welcome.

1 Look and circle. Say.

①

This is my (grandma) / dad.

She's **sad** / **happy**.

②

This is my **brother** / **mom**.

He's **cold** / **hot**.

③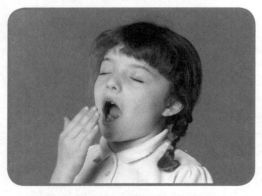

This is my **brother** / **sister**.

She's **hungry** / **tired**.

④

This is my **mom** / **dad**.

He's **happy** / **sad**.

8 Review

1 Look and draw. Say.

She's tired.

He's hot.

He's happy.

She's noisy.

Revision 4

1 Look and make a ✓ or an ✗. Say.

① brother ✓
sister ✗

② mom ☐
sister ☐

③ mom ☐
dad ☐

④ brother ☐
grandpa ☐

⑤ dad ☐
grandpa ☐

⑥ mom ☐
grandma ☐

2 Follow and circle. Say.

① ② ③ ④ ⑤

noisy   sad   cold   (noisy)   fast
quiet   happy   hot   quiet   slow

3 Look and circle.

1 This is my grandpa.

2 This is my sister.

3 This is my dad.

4 This is my grandma.

4 Look and number.

1 She's cold.   2 He's hungry.   3 She's happy.

4 He's sad.   5 She's hot.   6 He's tired.

      1

Easter

1 Look and number. Say.

1 egg   **2** flowers   **3** basket   **4** bunny

☐   1   ☐   ☐

2 Color the eggs. Draw and color a pattern.

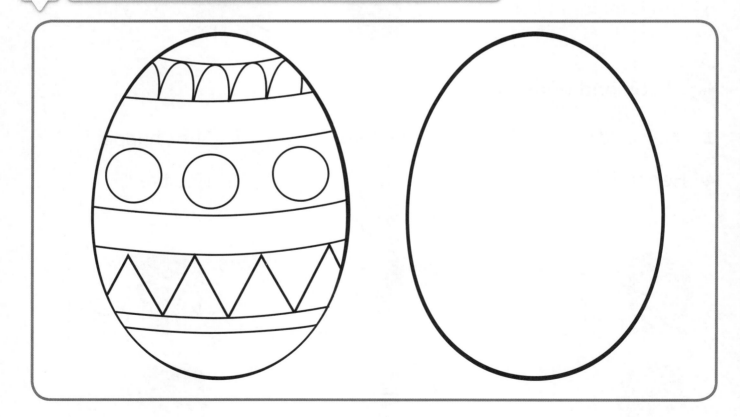

Vocabulary egg, flowers, bunny, basket

3 Look, count, and write the number. Say.

1

☐

☐

☐

1 Circle the odd one out. Say.

①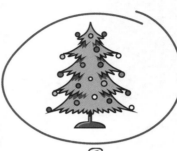

②

③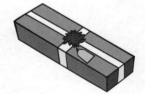

④

⑤

⑥

Vocabulary star, present, decoration, tree

2 Find and color.

Great Clarendon Street, Oxford, OX2 6DP, United Kingdom

Oxford University Press is a department of the University of Oxford.
It furthers the University's objective of excellence in research, scholarship,
and education by publishing worldwide. Oxford is a registered trade
mark of Oxford University Press in the UK and in certain other countries

ISBN: 978 0 19 403363 3

Printed in China

This book is printed on paper from certified and well-managed sources

ACKNOWLEDGEMENTS

Back cover photograph: Oxford University Press building/David Fisher

Cover Image: Gergana Hristova/Beehive.

Illustrations by: Bill Bolton/Advocate Art p.41 (animals); Andy Hamilton pp.8,
10, 16 (balloons), 19, 28, 35, 36 (African and Chinese mask), 37, 41 (boy and
girl), 42 (monkey puppet), 43 (animals), 45 (children), 49, 57, 59 (bottom), 60,
62; Gergana Hristova/Beehive pp.3, 6, 12, 20, 26 (story), 27 (objects), 34, 40,
48, 54 (story); Kelly Kennedy/Sylvie Poggio Artists pp.14 (paint splodges), 33, 50;
Andrew Painter pp.2, 4, 5, 7, 8 (objects on desk), 9, 11, 13, 14, 15, 16, 17, 18, 21,
23, 24, 25, 27 (boy and girl), 29, 30, 31, 32, 35 (boy and girl), 36 (funky mask),
38, 42 (animals), 43 (zoo), 44, 45 (animals), 46, 47, 51, 52, 53, 54 (boys, girls and
animals), 55, 58, 59 (top), 61, 63.

*The publishers would like to thank the following for permission to reproduce photographs
and other copyright material*: Getty Images pp.50 (smiling girl/KidStock), 60
(Easter eggs/selensergen); Graham Alder/MM Studios pp.7, 13, 21, 49 (girl),
55; MM Studios p.22 (car); Shutterstock pp.22 (toy building blocks/Ambient
Ideas, kite/italianestro, tree trunk/Masalski Maksim, train/Nykonchuk
Oleksii, beach ball/Olga Popova, tin cans/Roman Samokhin), 39 (monkey/
Alexander Dashewsky, hippo's hoof/Anan Kaewkhammul, lion/Anna
Omelchenko, giraffe/Brandon Seidel, zebra/Milena_, snake/Skynavin, hippo/
tantrik71, snake skin/Yuttasak Jannarong), 44 (penguin/Anton_Ivanov), 49
(unhappy boy/auremar, happy boy/Samuel Borges Photography), 50 (woman/
digitalskillet, portrait of happy senior couple/Monkey Business Images, man
smiling/Nadino, happy senior couple/T-Design), 56 (man with boy/Andy Dean
Photography, boy/eurobanks, girl/Gareth Boden, grandma/Voronin76), 60
(rabbit/pavla, chicken egg/pingu2004, daffodils/Samo Trebizan).